Liverpoc

The author is from ....pool family, though he grew up mainly on the Wirral. He now lives in London with his wife and two littl'uns. Like all Liverpool 'expats', he misses the place, and of course the good humour (and good-humoured-ness) of the people.

His grandfathers, Sammy and Solly, always had a quip or a funny story at the ready to make life more enjoyable, and this book is dedicated to them.

"A Birkenhead banker called Birrel" – see p80

Liverpool Limericks

Jerry Markison

with illustrations by
Dan Archer

Beauclair Books

First published in Great Britain in 2008 by
Beauclair Books
104 Amity Grove, London, SW20 0LJ
www.BeauclairBooks.co.uk

A CIP catalogue record for this book is available from the British
Library.

ISBN 978-0-9558843-0-6

All illustrations © Dan Archer 2008
www.archburger.com

Designed and typeset by Roger Davies
rogerdaviesdesign@btinternet.com

Printed and bound in Great Britain by
CPI Antony Rowe
www.antonyrowe.co.uk

Contents

Welcome to Liverpool!

At Lime Street there once was a porter
Who took longer for lunch than he oughter.
He'd knock off at ten
And was not seen again
For another five hours and a quarter!

Comedy Numbers

Old Doddy's so "tattyfilarious".
His talents are many and various:
He can sing, tell a joke,
Spread cheer to all folk,
And his tax return's bloody hilarious!

Trial by Water

A plumber with previous, Jock,
One day got a watery shock.
He fell off the Pier Head
And reflected with dread,
"I always go down from the dock!"

There Be Pirates!

Said a driver for George Henry Lee's,
"I earn a good living with ease."
(That's because when he can
From the back of his van
He also flogs bootleg CDs!)

Russell

I once had a girl from Fazakerley
Whose laugh was unbearably cackly.
So poor was my Sweets
She had tin foil sheets,
And when we made love it was crackly.

Stinking Rich

The Mersey made money, 'tis true,
Sending ships full of coal to Peru.
They returned full of turds
(Or "guano") of birds,
A cargo one shouldn't pooh-pooh!

The Bishopric

The Bish at the Wigwam of Paddy
Was known as a bit of a laddie.
He so often transgressed
With girls who confessed,
Kids called him not "Father" but "Daddy"!

Gambling Laws

On Saturdays Dave checked the scores
To see if he'd guessed all the draws.
Predicting just eight
Would have altered his fate
But the winner each week was John Moores!

In the Dog House

The mutt of a woman from Melling
Lost its nose in a fight by her dwelling.
She totally flipped
When the vet glibly quipped,
"At least this won't stop him from smelling!"

"You'll Never Walk Again!"

A yob in the Kop got excited
When Liverpool thrashed Man Utd.
He then got his hands
On a few of their fans,
A Double which left him delighted!

Modern Miracle

In a quaint little place, Raby Mere,
A boy once asked, "How am I here?"
Though he knew sexual theory
This *was* a good query
As both of his fathers were queer!

Non-Productive?

A bronchitic old bloke known as 'Wacker'

Was a failed computer code cracker.

He sat typing away

Smoking sixty a day

And confessed, "I'm a terrible hacker!"

Patriot Night

On St George's Day, Charlie from Chester

Met a girl, took her home and undressed her.

He had seen nothing finer,

Cried, "Vivat Regina!"

Then, thinking of England, possessed her!

The Literasy Our

A middle-class mother from Meols
At her daughter continually yeolls.
The girl's not a fool
But gets punished at school
Because of the way that she speolls.

Funny Guy

I heard of a person, O'Grady,

Whose story might strike you as shady.

He does what he can

To succeed as a man,

Having done very well as a lady!

Urban Regeneration

Aged thirty, a single Mum, Annie,
Said, "I'm ever so proud of my Fanny.
It's plain now to see
That she takes after me,
For she's finally made me a granny!"

Public Service Broadcasting

A lonely young lass called Ludmilla
Had features just like a chinchilla.
Her prospects weren't great
Till she went on Blind Date
And she's now very grateful to Cilla!

Inside Job

A gangster from Garston named Dale
Was known to be hard as a nail.
He had muscles, tattoos
And was skilful with screws,
Which is how he escaped Walton jail.

Cautionary Tail
(or Educating Rita)

At Knowsley Safari Park, Rita
From her Jaguar spotted a cheetah.
She was fixing a flat
On her motorised cat
As the real one proceeded to eat her!

Debt Collector

The shopping-obsessed Mrs Cohen
Into Town was addicted to goin'.
She'd buy stuff on tic
But the bills came so quick
She was always left owin' Owen Owen!

Oh Sh... Sugar!

Some Tate & Lyle operatives whined,
"Christ, this bloody factory's a grind!"
Blaspheming, the berks
Fell into the works
And emerged a good deal more refined!

Lets Pretend

An unscrupulous landlord from Eastham
Bought slums on the cheap and then leased 'em.
His service charge fees
Were a fraudulent wheeze
And if tenants complained he increased 'em!

"He's Got a Heart of Gold – Honest"

A lottery winner from Dingle
Has manners and skin rough as shingle.
He bores girls to death
And has rancid bad breath
Yet he hasn't, since winning, been single.

Occupational Hazard

Said a hooker from Widnes, "A thumb
Most weekends get shoved up my bum.
You feel a big knob
But it's part of the job –
That's what you expect in the scrum."

Close Family

A terrace-house down Scottie Road
Was a family of fourteen's abode,
Which they shared with a lodger
(A Welshman called Roger)
Three chickens, two goats and a toad!

Surprise, Surprise

I had a blind date with this Tina,
So we met by the Echo Arena.
Was it love at first sight?
Nah, I legged it in fright,
And you would have, too, if you'd seen 'er!

Proud Dad

"Our Kelly's fulfilled her ambition
To qualify as a beautician.
She does people's tans,
Their face, feet and hands
And leaves them in much worse condition!"

Made for the Job?

When standing for Birkenhead Mayor
Jim Hamilton thus did declare:
"I'll get drugs out of clubs
And close noisy pubs,"
But voters thought Hamilton square.

Seaman

A saucy old sailor of yore
Said, "The Mersey's a sight I adore:
The girls there are willing
(For under a shilling)
And soon I'll be coming ashore!"

Prankster

A call-centre worker named Sue
Took a call from a "Winnie the Pooh".
When he asked for her boss
She replied, at a loss,
"Bear with me, I'll just put you through!"

Ball Control

A fit Tranmere player called Guppy
Was dating an Albert Dock yuppie.
He liked his birds posh
And loaded with dosh,
While she valued skilled keepie-uppie!

Benefits and Drawbacks

Moaned an unemployed bloke from Old Swan,
"It's a full-time job just signing on!"
(He'd made dozens of claims
In differing names
As a highly skilled pro at this con!)

Who Is the Greatest Ever Liverpudlian?

Will Roscoe did much noble toil,

And Will Gladstone was a subject most loyal,

The Beatles were fab,

But for gift of the gab

The prize goes ("My arse!") to Jim Royle!

Plane Talking

John Lennon's big gob was unique.
He spoke with both wisdom and cheek.
He said, "Us four Scouse geezers
    Are bigger than Jesus!"
So it's right that he's honoured at Speke.

Practical Training

A Liverpool athlete called Clint,
As a youngster was constantly skint.
To afford to have fun
He'd pick pockets and run,
And that's how he'd learned how to sprint.

Opening Gambit

A slapper called Mary O'Dunnell
When out on the town to have fun'll
Make eyes at some guys
And manoeuvre her thighs
To the width of the Wallasey Tunnel!

Disconcerting

Pre-show at the famed Philharmonic
Some musicians swigged gin without tonic.
They played (Brahms and Liszt)
But were booed, jeered and hissed
For 'twas Weill – they messed up something chronic!

Age Before Beauty

A student at Liverpool Uni
Would frequently act like a loony.
He once stopped an old lady
And, sounding real shady,
Said, "Hi darlin', my name's Wayne Rooney!"

Very Comfortable

The Everton centre-midfield
Has a sponsorship deal all sealed.
Being sharp when he shoots
He's promoting some boots
So he's sure to be very well heeled!

Clinic Cynic

Said Rodney Street's leading physician,
"I'm an expert in men's micturition.
"To get well paid for this –
Daily taking the piss –
Is fulfilling my every ambition!"

Confused Signals

A DJ at Radio City
Mistakenly thought she was witty.
From her voice all her fans
In their lorries and vans
Mistakenly thought she was pretty!

No Luvvie Lost

One night on the Playhouse's stage
The actors stormed off in a rage
At the constant corrections
And vain interjections
When the prompter was on the wrong page!

No Sweat

Some say Lineker never played hard –
No ref ever showed him a card.
His most valuable role
Was to hang round the goal
And crisply tap in from a yard.

Life, Liberty and the Pursuit of Happiness (or Having a Riot)

Elaine lives in Liverpool 8.
She goes drinking most nights with her m8.
They wind up at Cream
Where they both have a scream
And go home in a god-awful st8!

Royal Visit
to the Car Factory at Halewood

The Union man was so cool
The Princess fell in love like a fool.
He refused to do much
About keeping in touch
And claimed he was working to rule!

Couple of Swells

A liner once crossed the Atlantic

As a storm made the waves grow gigantic.

A groom and his bride

Looked out from the side

And were sick, hand in hand - how romantic!

Art Appreciation

I once took a pal to the Walker,

Forgetting he's such a loud talker.

As we stood there to brood

On a big baroque nude

He 'whispered': "BY CHRIST, WHAT A CORKER!"

The Problem with Foreign Managers

Dalglish left opposing teams praying
He wouldn't dance through them when playing;
Then as Anfield's boss,
Left his own at a loss
As they never knew what he was saying!

Experiencing the Divine

From Hope Street there rises a tower,
A symbol of heavenly power,
Where clerics retire
With chaps from the choir
For a heavenly quarter of an hour!

Dogged by Bad Luck

A lad walked around Sefton Park
And climbed up a tree for a lark.
He slipped to the ground
And was mauled by a hound
Whose bite seemed much worse than the bark!

Too Much Media Exposure

When Cheggers appears on TV
He's as natural as ever could be.
This once led to failure
As Keith's genitalia
Was not what folks wanted to see!

A Heroine to Many

A young lady from Southport, Aretha,
Had always thought selling beneath her.
She now gets a buzz
From outwitting the fuzz,
Distributing drugs round Ibiza!

Getting Jumpy

Any steeplechase jockey with passion'll
Confirm how he loves the Grand National.
Any horse on the course
Will more often endorse
The view that it's rash – neigh - irrational!

Youngster's Own Goals

A scally skipped school for a week
To perfect his graffiti technique.
"Yer see," said the tyke,
"For Christmas I'd like
An ASBO slapped on by the beak!"

Golf Coarse

Ladies' Captain at Hoylake's great links
Was a lass who went in for high jinks.
On the seventeenth green
She did something obscene,
Which was par for the course for that minx!

Did That Glass Really Just Move?

One night down the pub Mike De Souza
Told a medium, "Mate, you're a loser!"
But Derek Acorah
Said, "I'm sensing an aura:
There's spirits, I'm sure, in this boozer!"

Beware the effects of the small Print

The police nicked insurance boss Bess
When found drunk in a state of undress.
With no hint of humility
She denied liability
As she claimed this was classed as 'excess'!

Chinatown

Wim Wang, who had roots in Hong Kong,
Said, "Liverpool's where I belong.
It's full of Chinese,
And life here's a breeze,"
But most people think that he's Wong!

Scenes from Everyday Life

To sit and watch Brookside was bliss,
A way of relaxing we'll miss.
The deaths, rapes and incest
All captured our interest,
As did watching young lesbians kiss!

All Play and No Work

A teenager, Jack, from Maghull
Looked constantly vacant and dull.
He said nothing at school,
For in class, as a rule,
His iPod was fixed to his skull!

Majorly Hot Currie

Edwina once penned a bestseller
About her affair with some feller.
She wrote, "Caution forbids
Any thoughts about kids,
For my eggs might contain salmonella!"

Organised Crime

The only posh house in Tuebrook
Proved too tempting for each local crook.
To get your own space
To burgle the place
You had to phone gangland and book!

"Woollyback's" Revenge

A "Taffy" residing in Wrexham
Is nice to folk if he respects 'em;
But if in the street
He happens to meet
Any Scousers, he nuts'em and decks'em!

Head and Shoulders above the Rest

When a red-shirted striker called Crouch
Gets close to the goal he must slouch.
For when scoring he might,
If at his full height,
Smack his face on the bar and yell, "Ouch!"

Effective Bedside Manner

A doctor who worked in Edge Hill
Was skilful at treating the ill.
Though no-one got better
They all signed a letter
Which added him into their will!

Animal Lover

A Birkenhead banker called Birrel

Fell deeply in love with a squirrel.

He explained from their nest:

"It's his nuts I like best!"

(There's nowt queer as folk on the Wirral!)

Comings and Goings

To Liverpool, back in its day,
The world and his wife came to stay.
'Twas not (more's the pity)
For love of the city
But a longing to get far away!

Factory Trip

A worker from Ellesmere Port

Enjoyed his job more than he ought.

He got very high

Within ICI

On the chemicals there he could snort!

Middle Ground

A Catholic from Newton-le-Willows
Seemed relaxed about mere peccadilloes.
Said she, "It's a sin
If a boy sticks it in,"
So she'd just jerk 'em off on the pillows!

It's not whether you win or lose…

(…It's whether Simon Cowell backs you or not)

A charming young chap called Ray Quinn

Entered X Factor hoping he'd win.

Leona's big voice

Was the natural choice

But Ray doesn't mind, he's quids in!

Satellite of Love

A space science student from Cheshire
Quite often felt stressed as a fresher.
But he found that depravity
With girls at low gravity
Would help him feel under less pressure!

Labour Pains

The Echo once printed a story
Which caused an almighty furore.
"Neil Kinnock," they said,
"Thinks Hatton's not Red
But a damaging underground Tory!"

Cleaning Up

Lord Leverhulme's wife used to josh,
"My hubby deserves all his dosh;
For it's thanks to his soap
One's permitted to hope
That the plebs have at last learned to wash!"

1207 - The Early Liverpool Scene

King John, on the "muddy pool's" strand,
Saw blokes busy down on the sand.
By trade they caught fish
But they told him their wish
Was really to be in a band!

Liverpool - Capital of Culture
(or Re: Branding)

The city's repute was unsavoury -
Known for riots and dock strikes and knavery.
Now it's won people's hearts
As a home to the arts
And fine buildings (most funded by slavery!)

Local Trivia

George Henry Lee (p.10) – a department store in Liverpool, first established as a bonnet warehouse in 1853 by Henry Boswell Lee on the same site as the modern store. Acquired by the John Lewis Partnership in 1940 but only recently rebranded John Lewis. **Owen Owen** (p.28) is another local department store name no longer seen on the High Street.

Guano (p.12) – The nitrates from the thousands of tonnes of bird dung brought from South America in the mid-19th century were used in the manufacture of fertilizer.

Halewood (p.56) – A major Ford production plant. Since 2002 it has been turning out X-type Jaguars and Freelander Land Rovers.

Hamilton Square (p.37) – Site of Birkenhead Town Hall, the square and surrounding streets bring to mind the handsome streets of Edinburgh's New Town. Not surprising perhaps, as that was what the landowner, Scottish shipbuilder William Laird (of Cammell Laird fame) commissioned Edinburgh architect James Gillespie Graham to do in the mid 1820s.

Hope Street (p.61) – A road that runs between the vast Anglican cathedral and the Liverpool Metropolitan Cathedral (Catholic), a.k.a. **Paddy's Wigwam** (p.13).

John Moores (p.14) – Born 1896 (Eccles), died 1993 (Formby). The founder of the Littlewoods Football Pools and retail empire. Chairman of Everton FC in the 1960s and 70s.

Liverpool Polytechnic was renamed Liverpool John Moores University in 1992.

The Kop (p.16) – The home fans' end at Liverpool FC's Anfield ground. Named after the Boer War battle of Spion Kop (1900) in which many from the Liverpool area lost their lives.

Lord Leverhulme (p.88) - The industrialist and philanthropist William Hesketh Lever (1851-1925), later Viscount Leverhulme (Hulme was his wife's family name), mass-produced "Sunlight Soap" at his model manufacturing community in Port Sunlight on the Wirral. This was a globalised business of the Victorian age: within ten years of its launch the soap was being sold in 134 countries and Leverhulme sourced his palm oil from plantations in the West Indies and the Congo (though his philanthropic inclinations did not prevent him from making use of forced labour). He founded the Lady Lever Art Gallery at Port Sunlight and endowed the School of Tropical Medicine in Liverpool. His company, Lever Brothers, merged with a Dutch company in 1930 to form Unilever.

Liverpool 8 (p.55) – City district incorporating Toxteth. Scene of the so-called 'race riots' of 1981, which contributed to the abolition of police powers to stop and search on the basis of suspicion only, excessive use of which had caused tension with the local black community.

Scottie Road (p.33) – Familiar name for Scotland Road, a (formerly) densely inhabited area north of the city centre with a large migrant and working class community. Singer and TV presenter **Cilla Black** (p.24) was a 'Scottie Roader'.

Speke airport (p.43) – Renamed Liverpool John Lennon airport in 2001.

Wacker (p.19) – A Scouse word, sometimes shortened to 'wack', meaning 'pal' or 'mate'. **'Scally'** (p.66) is another local word and means something like 'young rascal'. Liverpudlians are called **Scousers** (pp.43, 77) after a traditional, basic, local dish called scouse (or lobscouse), which is a stew of lamb or beef with potatoes, onions, carrots and swede, often served with pickled beetroot or red cabbage and white bread and butter. A vegetarian version is called 'blind scouse'.

William Gladstone (p.42) – Famous Victorian Liberal politician, who served four terms as Prime Minister. He was born in Liverpool in 1809 in **Rodney Street** (p.50), an elegant road associated with the medical profession, rather like London's Harley Street. Died 1898.

William Roscoe (p.42) – Lived 1753-1831. Little remembered outside his home town, this was a man of many parts. He was a noted historian, poet and lawyer, not to mention a banker, agriculturist and a Liverpool MP. His collection of early Italian and Dutch art – sold when the banking business took a turn for the worse - was the foundation of the **Walker Art Gallery** (p.58). He campaigned for decades against the Slave Trade, risking his life in a town where so many had vested interests in its continuance.

Index of First Lines

Do you know any limericks or other comic verses about Scousers or local culture? Fancy penning something yourself? Don't keep your satire to yourself – share it with the rest of us.
Log on to www.Liverpool-Limericks.co.uk